The Harlem Globetrotters

and Basketball's Funniest Games

The Harlem Globetrotters and Basketball's Funniest Games

by CLARE and FRANK GAULT

Illustrated by CHARLES McGILL

SCHOLASTIC BOOK SERVICES

NEW YORK · TORONTO · LONDON · AUCKLAND · SYDNEY · TOKYO

ISBN: 0-590-03000-0

Text copyright © 1976 by Clare S. Gault and Frank M. Gault. Illustrations copyright © 1976 by Charles McGill. All rights reserved. Published by Scholastic Book Services, a division of Scholastic Magazines, Inc.

12 11 10 9 8   1 2 3 4 5 6/8

Printed in the U.S.A.

For Kathy, Chip, Terrence, and Maureen

Basketball is fun to play. And there's one team that has more fun playing it than anybody — the Harlem Globetrotters.

They have tricky ways to pass the ball.

Other teams don't always find this
tricky ball-handling funny.
They get mixed up.

Globetrotters have fun
shooting baskets too.

And sometimes they fake a shot, just to
mix up the other team.

What's going on here? Is this basketball
or baseball?

It's just the Globetrotters clowning
around.

The Globetrotters always have a super-dribbler who can keep the ball away from the other team all by himself.

Why? So the rest of the Globetrotters can take time off to play a game of cards.

Sooner or later, a Globetrotter will get to take a free throw. But watch out. He may use a trick ball.

RUBBER BANDS

...BALL SNAPS BACK!

If the referee gets mad at their tricks, the Globetrotters know how to cool him off.

They may even try to cool off someone in the crowd. It looks like water, but it's only confetti. Were they surprised!

Passing, shooting, or playing funny tricks, the Globetrotters have more fun playing basketball than anybody.

Where did this crazy basketball team come from? How did it get started?

It all began many years ago in the city of Chicago, Illinois. It all began thanks to a man named Abe Saperstein.

Ever since he was a little boy, Abe Saperstein loved sports. He played baseball and basketball. But as Abe grew older, he didn't grow much taller. Even when he was a man, Abe was only five feet three inches tall. Abe was a good player, though, and he liked to help other players. So he became a coach.

One day someone told Abe about an all-black basketball team in the city. They needed a coach. Would Abe like the job? Abe said "yes."

People laughed when they saw Abe with his new team. Abe was white and very short. His players were black and very tall. But Abe was a good coach and soon they all became good friends.

Abe's team started to play basketball with other teams in the area. But not many people came to watch them. Soon the team ran out of money. It looked as if they would have to split up. But Abe had faith in his team. Somewhere people would come to watch them play.

Abe decided to look for other places outside the city of Chicago where the team could make a living. But first he made some changes. He took the team's old uniforms to his father's tailor shop and did a little work.

When Abe finished sewing, the uniforms looked different. There were gold stars on each shirt and a new name — "Harlem Globetrotters."

Abe thought "Harlem Globetrotters" was a good name. *Harlem* is the famous black section of New York City. Now people would know that this was an all-black team. And *Globetrotters* made it sound as if the team traveled around the world.

Actually, no one on the team was from Harlem. And none of them had ever been outside the United States. But travel they did — mostly to small towns all around the central part of the United States.

They all climbed into Abe's old car and
set out. Their first game was 50 miles west
of Chicago. They played a local team
there. Then they packed up and set out
again, looking for other teams to play.
They traveled all over — to Illinois, Iowa,
Nebraska, and other Midwest states.

At first, the Globetrotters were very serious. They didn't try to make people laugh. They were a great basketball team and they were out to prove it. They played hard to win. But sometimes that got them into trouble.

Once they were playing a team of lumberjacks in a small town. The lumberjacks were big and strong, but they were not good basketball players.

Before long, the score was: Globetrotters 112, Lumberjacks 5.

The Globetrotters didn't like such a one-sided game. And neither did the home-town crowd. They were angry. They didn't like to see their team getting clobbered.

So instead of shooting more baskets and scoring more points, the Globetrotters started doing tricks with the basketball. They passed the ball between their legs, over their shoulders, and under their arms. They bounced the ball off their heads, elbows, knees, and ankles. They put on a five-man juggling act.

The crowd laughed and enjoyed the action. The Globetrotters turned a dull game into something fun to watch.

As they traveled around, one-sided games happened often. When they did, the Globetrotters went into their act of doing tricks and clowning around. And the crowds loved it. After a while, the Globetrotters did tricks whether it was a one-sided game or not.

3 FT.

But some of their funniest games were not part of any act. Some of the places they visited didn't have regular basketball courts. They had to play in whatever place was there.

In one small town, the Globetrotters played the local team in a swimming pool that had been drained of water. The local team played there all the time, and they were used to it. But it was a new experience for the Globetrotters. Like most pools, the floor slanted upward from the deep end to the shallow end.

For the first half of the game, the Globetrotters had to move the ball uphill. That was hard work, so the Globetrotters slowed the game down. But at the half, the teams changed goals. Now the Globetrotters were moving downhill, so they speeded things up. The Globetrotters won the game.

In another place, the game was played in the hay loft of a big barn. And that was OK. But during the game, one of the Globetrotters came charging down the court so fast he couldn't stop. There was a door at the end of the barn where hay was lifted up and into the loft. The Globetrotter sailed right out that door.

The player fell twenty feet and landed in a pile of cow manure. Luckily, only his feelings were hurt. And a good bath took care of his other problem.

One night, it was very cold and the Globetrotters were playing in a long, narrow hall. To keep the place warm, there was a pot-bellied stove at each end of the hall. When one of the Globetrotters jumped for a rebound, he came down on one of the stoves.

The Globetrotter ran for the nearest bucket of water, his pants smoking. He wasn't hurt, and everybody called him the hottest basketball player in the world.

In those early days, the Harlem Globetrotters had five players plus Abe Saperstein, manager and coach. Once in a while, one of the regular players got sick or hurt. Then Abe Saperstein went into the game. He was their only substitute.

Abe was a good ball-handler and he had a very good two-handed set shot, so he did well even though he was so short. Besides, he had four other Globetrotters on the court with him.

The Globetrotters moved from town to town. The more they played, the better they became, and the more clowning they did.

Once in a while, a team they played got mad at their tricks.

"You can't play regular basketball," they would say to the Globetrotters. And then the Globetrotters would show them.

One time when this happened, the Globetrotters decided to let one man do all their shooting. They kept giving the ball to just that one man.

Even then, the other team couldn't stop them. The one Globetrotter scored 75 points and the Globetrotters won easily. The other team felt very foolish.

Traveling around to small towns and playing local teams was a hard way to make a living. The crowds were small and the Globetrotters didn't make much money.

But after a while, they got a big chance. There was a tournament to be played in Chicago. Eight teams would play each other and the winning team would be called champion. The tournament was all set, but one more team was needed. Abe Saperstein got the Globetrotters into the tournament as the eighth team.

The other teams didn't take the Globetrotters seriously. They thought the Globetrotters were just a bunch of clowns.

But the Globetrotters showed them.
They won every game they played. And
they won the tournament. Suddenly, the
Globetrotters were famous. They could
start playing big-name teams in large
cities.

The Globetrotters played the College
All-Stars. This was a team made up of all
the best players just out of school. The
game was played in the Chicago Stadium
before 22,000 fans. The Globetrotters lost
the game by two points in overtime, but
they proved they were a great team.

Years later, the Harlem Globetrotters played a number of games with another College All-Star team. This time the Globetrotters won 13 out of 18 games.

During all these games, the Globetrotters kept their sense of humor. They passed the ball between the All-Stars' legs. They shot baskets while sitting down. They rode to the basket piggyback. They used all the tricks in their bag. The crowds loved it. They saw great basketball and they had fun watching.

Today, the Globetrotters don't play the College All-Stars. They don't play other top professional teams as they did years ago. Their games are more of a show now. They spend more of their time and energy on making people laugh.

Most of the time, the Globetrotters play a team coached by Red Klotz. He's a good coach and many of his players have moved into the big leagues. For the sake of the show, Red's teams almost always lose to the Globetrotters. But they play other teams too — and almost always win.

Many famous players have been Harlem Globetrotters. Wilt Chamberlain started his professional playing career as a Globetrotter. Later, he led the Los Angeles Lakers to several championships in the NBA (National Basketball Association). He still says his time with the Globetrotters was the happiest of his life.

Nat "Sweetwater" Clifton also started as a Globetrotter. Later, he joined the New York Knicks and helped them win three championships.

And Bob Gibson was a Globetrotter who switched over to pitching baseballs for the St. Louis Cardinals. He became one of the best right-hand pitchers in National League history.

The Harlem Globetrotters have lived up to their name too. Forty years after they were formed, the team finally did play a game in New York's Harlem.

And they have been trotting the globe — they have gone completely around the world three times. They have played in more than 80 countries and traveled millions of miles. Every year, they play and travel around Europe. The Harlem Globetrotters are probably the best known sports team in the whole world.

The Globetrotters have a theme song. It's "Sweet Georgia Brown," a bouncy tune played while the team warms up before a game.

The beat of "Sweet Georgia Brown" seems to match the Globetrotters' style. The team forms a circle and practices their fancy passing — off the elbows, over the head, around the back. Fake one way, throw another. Rapid-fire ball handling. It's almost like a game of "hot potato" or "beanbag."

The Globetrotters can handle a basketball as if it were a toy. Bounce. Bump. Fake. Pass. And all the time their tune, "Sweet Georgia Brown," keeps bouncing along with them. Once you've heard it and watched the Harlem Globetrotters do their stuff, you'll know it forever.

And from then on, every time you hear their song and see them bounce onto the court, you can just bet that you're about to see the fastest, the greatest, the funniest basketball game in the whole world.

Big dates in the Globetrotters' history

Abe Saperstein coaches all-black team in Chicago	1926
Abe starts Harlem Globetrotters	1927
Globetrotters win World's Professional Basketball Tournament in Chicago	1940
Globetrotters play first game with College All-Stars but lose in overtime	1940
Globetrotters play series of games with College All-Stars and win 13 out of 18 games	1950
Globetrotters take first round-the-world tour	1952
Globetrotters play first game in Harlem, New York City	1968
Globetrotters play 10,000th game	1970
Globetrotters star in television series, *The Harlem Globetrotter Popcorn Machine*	1974

A Globetrotter photo album

The Globetrotters started with five regular players. After a while, two more players joined the team. Those original Globetrotters stopped playing years ago. And other players have taken their places. In fact, over the years more than 270 players have been Harlem Globetrotters.

But some things never change — the Harlem Globetrotters still have the fastest ball-handling, the craziest ways of shooting baskets, the most fun playing. Globetrotter games are still the funniest games in basketball.

Coach Abe Saperstein poses for a picture with six of his Globetrotters in 1963. This was 36 years after he had formed the first Harlem Globetrotter team.

Reece "Goose" Tatum was a great clown. He had an easy smile and huge hands. And he knew how to make people laugh. He was one of the most popular Globetrotters in the 1950's.

Fred "Curly" Neal is a super-dribbler. He can bounce the ball so fast it's hard to keep track of it.

UPI

Meadowlark Lemon can hold a basketball as if it were a grapefruit.

UPI

UPI

Wilt "The Stilt" Chamberlain got his start playing with the Globetrotters. Here he shows how to pass the ball over the shoulder. This picture was taken in 1960.